T0106270

Five Fun Plays for Christian Kids

• • • • • • • • •

Including Two Christmas Plays

Phyllis Flagg

WestBow
PRESS
A DIVISION OF THOMAS NELSON

WestBow Press books may be ordered through booksellers or by contacting:

WestBow Press
A Division of Thomas Nelson
1663 Liberty Drive
Bloomington, IN 47403
www.westbowpress.com
1-(866) 928-1240

Because of the dynamic nature of the Internet, any web addresses or links contained in this book may have changed since publication and may no longer be valid. The views expressed in this work are solely those of the author and do not necessarily reflect the views of the publisher, and the publisher hereby disclaims any responsibility for them.

Any people depicted in stock imagery provided by Thinkstock are models, and such images are being used for illustrative purposes only.

Certain stock imagery © Thinkstock.

ISBN: 978-1-4497-3151-9 (sc)

Library of Congress Control Number: 2011960575

Printed in the United States of America

WestBow Press rev. date: 11/22/2011

To my family who reads my plays, laughs at my jokes, builds my props, comes to my performances, and always supports me in whatever crazy scheme I dream up.

To my students who share their ideas and funny stories with me. Their imaginations have given me a wealth of material that I can use to create plays for everyone's enjoyment.

CONTENTS

THE CONTEST AT MOUNT CARMEL

THE CONTEST AT MOUNT CARMEL

· ·

The Contest at Mount Carmel is the story of Elijah and King Ahab. Elijah is a prophet of God, and Ahab is a wicked king. They have a contest to see whose god is the true God. This play is suitable for ages from fourth grade to adult.

Characters

Elijah (a prophet)
King Ahab
Queen Jezebel (Ahab's Wife)
Guard
Prisoner
Narrator
Servants

The Voice of the Lord
Several Prophets of Baal
Widow Woman
Two people to carry the ravens
One person with a horse costume

Props

- Background scenery for the palace, wilderness, mountain, and throne room. (A painted sheet can be hung behind the actors as background scenery)
- Several shrubs, or bushes (Cut from cardboard so that they stand up, or use artificial plants)
- A blue river (can be a colored strip of posterboard)
- Wagon (chariot)
- Whip (Stick with a string tied on the end)
- Binoculars
- Horse costume (Can be a papier mache or poster board horse head worn by the person who pulls the chariot. Drape the person in a brown blanket for the rest.)
- Cardboard bricks for the altar of the prophets of Baal
- Papier Mache stones for Elijah's altar (For the altars, a box painted with stone outlines or brick outlines can also be used instead.)
- Poster of fire or flames for Elijah's altar
- Buckets (1-3)
- Ravens (2) (can be made from posterboard or papier mache)
- Small pieces of bread for the ravens
- Several small sticks (for widow woman)
- Table and bowls for making bread
- Tissues
- Plastic water bottles for prophets of Baal

THE CONTEST AT MOUNT CARMEL

SCENE I: AHAB'S PALACE

Narrator: "Once there was a king named Ahab. He became famous for something that most people don't want to be famous for. The Bible says he did more things to make God angry than anyone ever did before in the whole history of man. That's when the Lord decided to send Elijah to bring Ahab a message. Not just any message, mind you, but a message of God's punishment. Do you think he was happy to hear it? Listen and find out."

(King Ahab is seated on the throne.)

(Guard escorts a prisoner before the king. The prisoner kneels, begging for mercy.)

Prisoner: "Mercy, O King. I'm innocent!"

King Ahab: "Guilty. Sentenced to 100 years in prison. Take him away!" *(King waves his hand indifferently)*

Guard: "Yes, Sire."

(Guard escorts the unlucky prisoner away.)

King Ahab: "Send the next complainer in. Hurry up, so I can throw him in jail and get to my dinner."

Elijah: "O King Ahab, the Lord God of Israel wants you to know that it's not going to rain for a long, long time. You've made God so angry that He is going to stop the rain until you are sorry. Your crops will die, your animals will die, and if you don't repent, you will die too!"

King Ahab: *(Gets up and walks back and forth angrily)* "What? How dare you enter my court with this news? I'm so angry I can't even think of a good punishment for…hey, where did he go?"

(While the king is talking, he turns away and Elijah walks off, unnoticed.)

(Queen Jezebel yells from offstage, "Ahab!", then marches onstage).

Queen: "Ahab! You're late for dinner! I've prepared a feast and the roast leg'o'lamb is getting cold."

King Ahab (*looking frightened*) "I'm sorry. Don't yell at me. I can't stand it when you yell at me. I just had a mean prophet in here yelling at me too."

Queen: "And you let him get away? Was it that horrible Elijah? He says terrible things about me. I can't imagine why. I'm a perfectly wonderful queen, aren't I?" (*Ahab nods quickly*) "Why didn't you have him speared, or dragged behind my chariot, or something?"

King Ahab: "I don't know how he got away. I was talking, and then, suddenly, he was gone."

Queen: "If I want something done right, I have to do it myself. I'll get him next time he dares to show his face!" (*She shakes her fist menacingly.*)

SCENE II: OUTSIDE THE PALACE

Narrator: "Elijah walked outside the palace, and as soon as he finished speaking, the Lord spoke to him."

Lord's voice: "Elijah, go hide by the brook of Cherith. I will send some special messengers to feed you."

Narrator: "The Lord promised to care for him during the time of no rain. So Elijah ran to the brook. He ran…and he ran…and he ran some more." (*Elijah jogs around the stage*) "Man, he was tired from all that running! But Ahab didn't find him. And neither did Jezebel. When he reached the river at last, he flopped down on the bank," (*Elijah drops down, exhausted*) "and rested for the night. In the morning, he looked up."

(*Two black birds, carried by children, swoop down close to his head*)

Elijah: "What's that? Ravens? Shoo! Shoo! Wait, what's that you have in your mouth? A piece of bread? For me? Thanks, I'm starving." (*He takes the bread and pretends to eat it.*) "Those must be the special messengers that God promised to send."

Narrator: "And the ravens came every morning…" (*Ravens fly onstage again with bread*)

Narrator: "And every evening…" (*Ravens fly onstage with more bread*)

Narrator: "Until the brook finally dried up."

(*Elijah crawls over to get a drink from the brook.*)

Elijah: "No more water in the brook. (pant, pant) I'm so thirsty."

Lord's voice: "Elijah, get up and go to Zarephath. I have a widow woman there who will feed you."

SCENE III: OUTSIDE THE TOWN OF ZERAPATH

Narrator: "So Elijah went to Zarephath. It was a long….hot…dusty…walk." (*Elijah walks around stage.*) "When he came to the gate of the city, he saw a woman picking up sticks. He wondered if that was the woman God had spoken of. He walked over to talk to her."

Elijah: "Hello, would you please, *(pant, pant)* fetch me a little water? I'm really *(pant, pant)* thirsty."

Woman: "Yes, yes, of course. Wait right here."

Elijah: "Oh, please, before you go, could you bring me a piece of bread too? I haven't eaten for days."

Woman: "Well, I don't have anything except a bit of flour and a little oil. It's only enough to make a small biscuit, and I'm going to cook it for my son and myself, and after that, it's curtains for us! Boo-hoo, boo-hoo." (*She sobs loudly*)

Elijah: (*Hands her a tissue. She blows her nose loudly.*) "Don't worry. It's not going to be curtains for any of us. Go make the small bit of bread, and give it to me first."

Woman (*turns to audience*) "Did he say, 'give it to him first'? What is he thinking?"

Elijah: "It will be all right. God is going to feed us until the rain comes again."

Woman: "Well, ok, if you say so. I'll do it for the Lord. But I hope you're right."

(*The woman goes over to a table and begins making the bread.*)

Narrator: "And Elijah was right. Every time the woman made a new cake of bread, the flour and the oil appeared again right away."(*Woman looks down into the bowl, then up at the audience with a look of surprise.*) "They all had enough to eat and drink. One day, the Lord came and spoke again to Elijah."

Lord's voice: "Elijah, go back to the king, and tell him that I'm going to send rain soon."

Narrator: As Elijah journeyed toward the palace, King Ahab came out to meet him in his chariot.

SCENE IV: ON THE ROAD TO THE PALACE

(Elijah walks across the stage. King Ahab rides in on a wagon pulled by his "horse")

Ahab: *(Carriage stops, and he stands up.)* "So, there you are! Where have you been hiding? You're the cause of all these problems. What do you have to say for yourself, you troublemaker? You better start shaking in your boots when I'm talking!" *(He shakes his whip menacingly.)*

Elijah: "You're the troublemaker, King Ahab! And I'm going to prove it. Go get your evil prophets of Baal, and meet me at the mountain called Mount Carmel!"

Ahab: *(in a whiny voice)* "Don't tell me what to do! I'm the king." *(He drops his whip, and when he bends down to pick it up, Elijah slips behind a bush and walks away.)* "Hey, where did he go? He always gets away from me somehow. Jezebel's going to kill me. Guard! Come here immediately!"

Guard: *(steps out from the back of the chariot)* "Yes, Sire. What do you command?"

Ahab: "Go around the whole country, and tell everybody that I'm going to make a fool of Elijah the prophet. Tell them all to come and watch! Hurry up, now, I'm late for dinner again!"

(King Ahab rides off in his chariot.)

SCENE V: ON THE MOUNTAIN

Narrator: "So Ahab gathered all the false prophets and went up on the mountain. All the people of the country came to see what would happen, and whose god was the true God."

Ahab: "Go on, Elijah! Start the show!"

Elijah: "People of Israel! How long will you wait to choose your God? If Baal is the true god, then serve him, but if the Lord God of Israel is the true God, then choose Him. Make up your minds today!"

Narrator: "The prophets of Baal went first. They made an altar and prayed to their god, Baal, to send down fire." (*Prophets of Baal pile up bricks into an altar, or pretend to, and pray as they jump and dance around it*) "Nothing happened. They prayed all day, but still, nothing happened. They jumped…and they cried… and they danced around the altar, but still nothing happened. They were so exhausted, they had to stop for some refreshments."

(*A servant brings out water bottles to the exhausted prophets who fall down on the ground. They drink greedily.*)

Elijah: "What's wrong over there? Isn't your god listening? Maybe he's talking to someone, or taking a trip. Maybe he's sleeping! (*King Ahab makes an angry face at his prophets.*) Why don't you yell louder and wake him up?"

Narrator: "The prophets finally gave up." (*Prophets look at each other, then at audience, shrugging their shoulders.*) "It was Elijah's turn. He built an altar out of stones." (*Elijah builds the altar, or pretends to, as the narrator speaks.*) "He asked the servants to pour water on his altar, lots and lots of water. That's unusual for someone who wants to start a fire, don't you think?" (*Servants come out with buckets and pretend to pour water on the altar.*)

Elijah: "Lord, please hear me, and show these people that you are the true God."

Narrator: "And fire came down and licked up all the water around the altar." (*A poster of flames appears above Elijah's altar.*) "And the people knew that the Lord was the true God. And they killed the false prophets." (*False prophets run off the stage.*)

Elijah: "Ahab, get in your chariot, because you're about to get really wet. The rain's a comin'!" (*Thunder and rain sounds.*)

Narrator: "And Ahab hurried into his chariot, and Elijah ran ahead of him to the town of Jezreel, for the Lord gave him extra running power."

(*King Ahab rides his chariot. Elijah runs behind him, overtaking him and runs easily faster than the chariot all the way around the stage and off.*)

Narrator: "Meanwhile, back at the palace…"

(*Scene opens to Jezebel sitting on her throne. A guard enters and whispers in her ear.*)

Jezebel: "What? He killed all my prophets? I'm going to make mincemeat out of that Elijah when I find him! Get my chariot!"

7

SCENE VI: IN THE WILDERNESS

Narrator. "Jezebel combed the countryside, looking everywhere for Elijah. Elijah heard that Jezebel was after him, and she was worse than a hundred Ahabs, so he hid in the wilderness."

(Jezebel gets in the chariot. She rides around, carrying binoculars, looking everywhere for Elijah. Meanwhile, Elijah hides behind every bush, dodging her. Finally she goes back to the palace, leaving Elijah sitting in the wilderness, looking depressed.)

Lord's voice: "Elijah, why are you hiding here?"

Elijah: "I'm hiding from that scary Jezebel. She's mean, and she's after me! There's nobody left in the whole world who believes in God besides me. I give up!"

Lord's voice: "Don't be afraid, Elijah. There are seven thousand people in Israel who still believe in Me. Go to Damascus, and I will give you a helper there, and you will be safe. I am going to choose a new king who will serve Me."

(Elijah walks off stage, smiling.)

Narrator: "And Elijah found his helper, Elisha, and the others who served God, and lived happily ever after doing great miracles, until one day, a chariot of fire came down and… but wait, that's…another story."

Optional Ending: Students could recite, or Narrator could read the poem on the following page at the end or beginning of the play. Students could draw scenes as described in the play, and show them like a slide show during the recitation.

Elijah the Tishbite

Elijah, called "The Tishbite" was a prophet sent from God
To go to old King Ahab, the mighty king who trod–
In evil ways, in doing wrong, he was the worst of all.
Elijah went to tell him, "You're headin' for a fall."

Old Ahab shook with anger when Elijah said, "NO RAIN
Is coming to the kingdom until your people claim
That my God is the true God; He's the only one to serve.
But 'til that day, no rain at all is just what you deserve."

Ahab tried to kill him, but Elijah ran and stayed
Beside the brook of Cherith. His dinner there was made
By ravens, bringing crumbs of bread, obeying God's command.
They carried bits right to him, and dropped them in his hand.

One day the brook dried up, as dry as old dead bones.
Elijah prayed to God and cried, "I'm out here all alone."
"Don't be afraid," the Lord told him. "I know a woman well
Who'll give you food and water, and a cozy place to dwell.

So Elijah went to see her; one cake was all she had.
"Give that cake to me," he said, "And things won't be so bad."
And every time she poured the flour, it came back in the bowl.
And every time she checked the pot, it still was full of oil.

One day King Ahab chanced to meet Elijah on the road.
"Let's have a test," he said, "and see what tales will be told
About the Mount of Carmel. We'll have a contest there
And all the world will watch and see which God does rule the air."

King Ahab's prophets prayed and cried to the false god they named Baal.
All day long they jumped and danced, and loudly did they wail.
But nothing fell, no fire blazed, and nothing did they hear
Except Elijah asking them, "Has your god closed his ears?"

Then came Elijah's turn. He said, "Pour water all around.
I want to see it running down and soaking up the ground."
Then to the Lord he prayed just once, and fire fell so fast
It licked the water up and burned the wood right into ash.

"Your God must be the true one," King Ahab had to say.
And all the people worshipped God–O, what a glorious day!
"Get your chariot, Ahab," Elijah warned in glee.
"It's going to rain more rain than you and I have ever seen.

The clouds began to gather on the horizon late that day.
Then came the rain, and Ahab in his chariot raced away.
But Elijah ran much faster, and as the raindrops poured–
God proved to one and all that day that He's the One True Lord.

(★The Contest at Mount Carmel can also be adapted and used as a Christmas program. Here are additional lines to adapt the poem.)

THE CONTEST AT MOUNT CARMEL
(Adapted for a Christmas Theme)

Grandmother: "Children, gather round! It's almost time to open our presents!"

(Children gather around her, seated on the floor.)

Child 1: "Tell us a story, Grandma. Tell us about something in the Bible."

Grandmother: "I've told you about the Christ child who was born on Christmas many years ago. But do you know why that special baby was sent from God?"

Child 2: "So we could worship Him?"

Grandmother: "Yes, that's true, but there's more to it than that. God had to send Jesus because people needed to learn about God. Jesus came to tell us all about His Heavenly Father, and about sin, and how to believe in God."

Child 3: "Couldn't they read about Him in their Bible?"

Grandmother: "They didn't have any Bibles in the old days. They had to listen to the prophets. Prophets tried to warn people to obey God, but the people didn't always listen. There was a lot to do before the Jewish people were ready for the Messiah to come."

Child 4: "Tell us about a prophet, Grandmother, pleeease."

Grandmother: "Well, let's see. My favorite prophet was Elijah. He was born during the time of a very wicked king named Ahab. The people had forgotten about God. Elijah had a dangerous job. He had to tell the king that God was angry with him. Let's go into the den and I'll finish telling you the story."

(Grandmother and children exit. Then, continue with THE CONTEST AT MOUNT CARMEL *play. At the end of the play, add in the next scene.)*

Child 1: "That was a great story!"

Grandmother: "Yes, there are many Bible stories that prepared the way for Jesus to come. Finally He was born in Bethlehem, and when He grew up, He died on the cross to save us from our sins. Have you asked Jesus into your heart already?"

Children: *(shout together)* "Yes!"

(Children or choir begins to sing "Joy to the World".)

THE CHRISTMAS JOURNEY

· · · · · · · · · · · · · · · · · · · ·

THE CHRISTMAS JOURNEY

In The Christmas Journey, a news reporter, along with his cameraman, has been transported to Bethlehem on the very same day that Christ was born. After getting over the initial shock, the reporter decides to take advantage of his situation, and record the events that occur on that special day. In the process, he learns the importance of the Savior's birth, and the effect it had on the world.

Characters:

Carl Frank (a reporter)   Shepherd 1
Jeff Black (a cameraman)   Shepherd 2
Narrator   Shepherd 3
Aaron (a traveler)   Angel 1
Joseph   Angel 2
Mary   Choir (Bell choir or singing)
Innkeeper   Several townspeople

Props

- Costumes for Bible times (townspeople, traveler, innkeeper, shepherds, angels, Mary and Joseph)
- A video camera
- Cloth to cover the camera
- Notepad and pen
- Fan
- Scattered papers
- A bundle for the traveler to carry
- Pots and pans
- Small table
- Shepherd staff
- Manger
- Straw
- Baby Jesus wrapped in a blanket or strips of cloth
- Giant star
- Campfire (can be made from posterboard and sticks)
- Bench or platform for angels
- Sheep
- Spear
- Suggested Songs: Silent Night, Away in a Manger (Taken from a hymnal). "A Carol for Today": from 4 Cool Carols 4 Cool Ways, by Dennis and Nan Allen "What Will Your Answer Be?" From Rock Solid: God's Promises for the Trail of Life, (Both songs are from : Dovetail Music and Lifeway/Worship.)

THE CHRISTMAS JOURNEY

. . . .

SCENE 1: BUSY STREETS

(The scene opens with two men lying on the floor, and the sound of a rushing wind. A video camera lies on the ground, as well as scattered papers, a notebook, and a pen. A fan blows wind upon the two men as they awaken.)

Carl: *(Sits up, dazed.)* "What a storm! Hey, Jeff, are you all right?" *(He shakes his friend. Jeff sits up slowly in the wind and brushes away papers that blow by him. The wind slows down and stops as Jeff looks around in wonder.)*

Jeff: "What happened? Where are we?"

Carl: "We're on the ground, that's where. There was a tornado, remember? It hit our studio. We were lucky to get out of there alive."

Jeff: "Yes, but *where* did we end up? This doesn't look right. Look around, Carl."
(Carl looks around. People are walking by, dressed in robes from Bible times. They stop and stare at the men, then make a wide circle to avoid them, whispering and pointing.)

Carl: *(Looks away from Jeff for the first time.)* "Must be a movie set. Someone's making a movie about Bible times. We must have landed on their set."

Jeff: "No, Carl, I think something's different. Listen to their words. They're not speaking English."

Carl: "You're right. It's Hebrew. Good thing I studied Hebrew at college. I'll translate for you...Everyone's complaining because Caesar Augustus has sent out a decree that all the world should be taxed...CAESAR AUGUSTUS! Why, he reigned over 2,000 years ago!"

Jeff: "That means....I think it means...uh...it can't be....but–"

Carl: "We've traveled through time! We're in the past. Get your camera ready. This is going to be the best story I've ever done! C'mon, let's go interview some people."

(A traveler, carrying a heavy burden upon his back, enters.)

Carl: "Excuse me, sir, where are you headed?" *(Cameraman follows behind, filming.)*

Traveler: (*Looks oddly at them, especially at the camera.*) "Aaron's the name, and I'm headed to Jerusalem. I was born there, you know. Why do we have to go back to where we were born? This is quite an inconvenience. I have much more important things to do than this. Excuse me!" (*Storms off.*)

Carl; "It seems that some travelers aren't enjoying their pilgrimage. Ah, here's another couple. You there, with the beautiful lady. What's your story?"

Joseph: "I haven't got time to tell you a story right now."

Carl: "I'll just take a moment of your time, I promise. What's your name?"

Joseph: "The name's Joseph, and this is my hometown. Now I really must go…my wife is just about to have a baby, and we must get to the inn."

Mary: "Hurry, Joseph. There's not much time now."

Carl: "But, just one more question…wait…"

(*Joseph and Mary hurry away. The news reporter shakes his head sadly.*)

Carl: "Well, I wish them the best of luck finding a room. It's not a good night for having a baby, although the stars are especially bright tonight. In fact, I don't remember seeing a night this clear and bright in a long time. There is a really bright star over that inn (*pointing*). Let's go over there and check it out."

(*Students sing "Silent Night", or play it on the tone chimes or bells.*)

SCENE II: AT THE INN

(*At the inn, the innkeeper is rushing around with pots and pans banging in his/her arms.*)

Carl: "Hello, Innkeeper. Busy night?"

Innkeeper: "Ahhh! Not another one! Not one more guest, do you hear? I'm full, no, I'm exploding with guests! My inn is the busiest in Bethlehem!" (*At the word "Bethlehem" Carl and Frank look at each other and whisper "Bethlehem"*) "People are sleeping on the floor, in the closets, under the tables…no more!"

Jeff: "We're not here for a room, sir." (*Carl looks at him, surprised. Jeff says, "I did my language homework too."*)

Innkeeper: "What? Who are you, then…robbers? Your clothes are very strange. And you're carrying a strange instrument, nothing that I've ever seen around here." (*Jeff puts the camera behind his back.*) "I have nothing to steal. All I have is pots and pans, and believe me, I know how to use them!" (*Shakes the pans at the newsman.*)

Jeff: "I'm not a robber! I'm a camera man, I mean, uh, we're-" (*Carl interrupts him before he can give away their identity. Jeff quickly covers the camera with a cloth he grabs from the table.*)

Carl: "We're scribes. I write things down. (*whispers to Jeff, "Give me a notepad." Jeff hands him one and he fishes in his pocket for a pen.*) "I'm writing about Bethlehem and the tax situation." (*He pretends to scribble on his pad.*)

Innkeeper: "I haven't got time for this. I've got to get my stew ready. Out of my way, there's someone at the door again! Oh me, oh my…"

(*Mary and Joseph stand at the door knocking.*)

Jeff: (*Speaking in Carl's ear*) "There's that poor couple again. The ones who are having the baby. Well, I mean, *she's* having the baby. Carl, do you think this is *THE* Bethlehem, you know, the one in the Bible?"

Carl: "Just keep the camera rolling. This is great stuff."

(*The innkeeper drops a couple of pans, muttering, then quickly snatches them up and hurries off to answer the door. The innkeeper opens the door, takes one look at them and says "No Room!"*)

Joseph: "But sir, my wife, she's having a baby. She can't have her baby out here in the street. We'll take anything, anything at all."

Innkeeper: (*sighs*) "I'm just too kind, yes, too kind for my own good. The only corner of space I have left is in the stable. You'll have to share with the animals. That's the best I can do, and I'm not kidding."

Joseph: "You're so kind to help us this way." (*The innkeeper looks at the audience and nods knowingly.*) "May the Lord bless you. Thank you." (*They all go offstage.*)

Narrator: "And so it was, that while they were there, the days were accomplished that she should be delivered. And she brought forth her firstborn son, and wrapped him in swaddling clothes, and laid him in a manger, because there was no room for them in the inn." (*All scripture quotes taken from the Holy Bible, King James Version.*)

(*Choir sings or plays "Away in a Manger"*)

SCENE III: THE HILLSIDE

Narrator: "And there were in the same country shepherds abiding in the field keeping watch over their flock by night."

(Carl and Jeff walk onto the scene, this time dressed in local clothing. Carl faces the camera and speaks. The camera is still covered with a cloth, exposing only the lens.)

Carl: "I'm standing on a quiet hillside near the town of Bethlehem. My associate and I have somehow traveled back through time. Something big is about to happen, and I'll be your eyes and ears. I'm going to ask these shepherds what they think of the crowds of people rushing to Bethlehem. Maybe they can shed some light from the local viewpoint."

(Shepherds are gathered around a campfire to keep warm.)

Shepherd 1: "It's time to check on the sheep again."

Shepherd 2: "You go this time. I went last time."

Shepherd 1: "It's too cold. My toes are numb."

Shepherd 3: "Oh, stop arguing. I'll go. You two are always fighting." *(Shepherd walks off.)*

Carl: "Hello, there, shepherds. How's it going out here on the hillside?"

Shepherd 2: "Who's there?" *(Jumps up and waves a staff wildly.)*

Carl: *(Steps back and dodges the staff.)* "I'm a scribe, and I'm here to talk with you."

Shepherd 1: "Well, it's not a good idea to sneak up on people in the dark. Last week, a bear came around in the dark, and I stabbed him with my spear, just like this." *(He thrusts his spear forward toward the reporter, who steps aside.)*

Shepherd 2: "Aw, that's nuthin. I killed a lion with my staff. I jumped on him, and wrestled him down and--"

Shepherd 1: "Man, you're always showing off. A bear is a lot bigger than a lion. I-"

(He is interrupted as Shepherd 3 returns.)

Shepherd 3: "Did you see that huge star? *(Points up)* I've never seen anything quite like it. It's fantastic!"

Shepherd 2: "It must be a brand new star! I've been out here every night, and I've never seen it before."

Shepherd 3: "A new star.....I remember reading something about a new star in the scroll of Isaiah. Or....was it Jeremiah? Anyway, a new star is supposed to appear when the Messiah has been born."

Shepherd 1: "There are a lot of promises about the Messiah. He's going to heal the sick, raise the dead, teach us about His Heavenly Father and much, much more. He's probably going to kick those Romans right out of Israel for good. We've been waiting for Him for almost two thousand years."

Shepherd 2: "It sure would be wonderful if we could meet Him in person. Hey, where's that light coming from? What's happening?"

(Lights grow brighter. Angels come on stage and step on a bench or platform above the shepherds. All kneel down before the angels.)

Narrator: "And lo, the angel of the Lord came upon them, and the glory of the Lord shone round about them, and they were sore afraid. And the angel said unto them, 'Fear not, for behold, I bring you good tidings of great joy, which shall be to all people.'"

Angel 1: "Don't be afraid. We bring good news. A special baby has been born."

Angel 2: "In the city of David, in a manger, you will find the baby. He is the Savior, Christ the Lord."

Angel 1: "He will save the people from their sins."

(Children or choir sings: "A Carol for Today").

(Angels leave.)

SCENE IV: THE MANGER

Carl: *(Speaks into the camera in a reverent tone.)* "We are following the shepherds to the town to find the baby. The angels said that the baby would be found in a manger. This is a very unusual story. If the baby is so special, what is He doing in a manger? It's a mystery we will try to unravel for our viewers."

(Shepherds enter from the back of the auditorium. They travel toward the stage.)

Shepherd 1: *(Points, and speaks with excitement.)* "There's the stable! I'm sure of it."

Shepherd 2: "How do you know?"

Shepherd 3: "Look at the star. It's right above the door. It's like a sign pointing the way."

(Shepherds kneel before the manger. Mary and Joseph kneel or stand beside the manger.)

Mary: "His name is Jesus."

Joseph: "The angel told me He would save His people from their sins."

Shepherd 3: "This is what we've all been waiting for; the birth of the Messiah."

Shepherd 2: "He's finally arrived. The prophecies have all come true. This will be the beginning of a new world."

Shepherd 1: "We must tell everyone about what we saw tonight. Let's spread the word that the Christ child is born."

(Children sing: "What Will Your Answer Be?")

Carl: "We've seen a miracle tonight. This night will go down in history. Jesus was born to save the world. And you've seen it all right here on TNN. We'll be following the story of this very special child, and it's sure to be something wonderful. This is Carl Frank, signing off."

(As they walk offstage, Jeff asks Carl) "Carl, got any ideas about getting home?"

Carl: "I'll think we'll stick around a few years. Many more amazing things are on the way. By the way, did you happen to bring a spare battery?"

(Closing song: "Joy To The World").

CHRISTMAS COURAGE

CHRISTMAS COURAGE

Christmas Courage is a play about a young boy who is nervous about performing in the Christmas play at his church. He even dreams of messing up the performance. By hearing the story of Gideon's victory in the Bible, he learns courage to help him perform.

Characters

Steve
Brian
Several young children
Teacher
Steve's mother's voice
Steve's dad
Angel

Gideon
Soldier One
Soldier Two
Girls' Choir or Children's Choir
Gideon's Men (several actors)
Narrator
Gideon's servants (1 or 2)

Props

- Piano book
- Piano
- Trumpet or other instrument for Brian to play
- Cot or small bed
- Small rhythm instruments for dream children
- Newspaper
- Chair
- Fleece (can use a fuzzy blanket tied in a bundle)
- Two Signs (Stars and moon for night, sun and clouds for morning)
- Tent for Soldier One and Two
- Horns for Gideon's soldiers
- Flashlights or lanterns
- Sheep
- Staff
- Binoculars

*Suggested Song: "Christmas Bell" is found in Majesty Hymns, a hymnal published by Majesty Music, Inc., P.O. Box 6524, Greenville, SC 29609, 1997.

CHRISTMAS COURAGE

．．

SCENE I: THE SCHOOL ROOM

(Scene opens as Steve walks onto the stage, carrying a piano book.)

Steve: "I guess I'll practice my Christmas song. It's only two weeks until the play." *(He walks to the piano, opens the book and begins to play. After playing several wrong notes, he says, "I give up!" and slumps down on a chair.)*

(Brian enters, carrying a trumpet.)

Brian: "Hey, Steve, what's up?"

Steve: "Oh, I've been trying to practice my song for the Christmas play, but I keep getting it wrong."

Brian: "I know how you feel. It took me a whole month to get my song right. Here's the part I had trouble with." *(He holds up his trumpet or instrument and plays a little of Hark, the Herald Angels Sing... Then he puts the horn down and says),* "See? I've got it now! You can do it too!"

Steve: "What if I mess up on the night of the play? Everyone's going to be watching me. I'll get nervous, and then…..crash….I'll hit the wrong notes again."

Brian: "The only thing I know to do is practice over and over until it gets easier. You'll get it eventually. Never give up, that's what my teacher says. Let's get going, the practice is about to begin."

(The two boys walk off the stage together.)

(Children enter and begin picking up their bells.)

Teacher: "Class, let's practice our first song for the play."

(Students play and/or sing: "Christmas Bell.)

SCENE II: STEVE'S HOME

(Steve comes on stage in his pajamas.)

Steve's Mother: *(calls from offstage)* "Good night, Steve. Pleasant dreams."

(Steve settles himself on the cot.)

Steve: "I hope I don't dream about the play again. That was a terrible dream I had last night."

(The lights dim, and the children walk slowly onto the stage, as if in a dream. They circle the cot, chanting.)

Dream Children: "Steve... Steve...get up, it's your turn to play your song."

Steve: *(Sits up and looks around in shock.)* "In my pajamas? Why didn't anyone tell me it was time for the play? I can't play in my pajamas!"

(Steve rushes over to the keyboard. He sits down, and begins to play. The children slowly pick up their instruments and walk toward him, banging their instruments loudly. He covers his ears, then gets up, trips up the steps, and the children follow him.)

Dream Children: "Steeeve... Steeeve...., where are you going? We need you to play for us."

(They follow him until he says back down on his cot. Then the children disappear quickly and he sits up. "Dreaming? I was dreaming again? I'll never survive this play!"

(Children go off stage. Dad enters, carrying a newspaper. He sits down to read, and Steve enters.)

Steve: "Dad, I'm really having a problem."

Dad: "What's that, son?"

Steve: "Well, it's about the play. I can't seem to get my song right. When I get in front of people, I get nervous, and then I hit all the wrong notes. I'm even having bad dreams about it."

Dad: "It's not unusual for someone to be nervous or afraid. Gideon was a judge of Israel, but when God told him to go to war, he was so afraid he couldn't sleep either."

Steve: "What did he do about it?"

Dad: "He had to learn to trust God. Come on with me. I'll show you a video about Gideon and what he did."

SCENE III: GIDEON'S HOME

Narrator: "In those days, the children of Israel did evil in the sight of the Lord, and the Lord delivered them into the hand of Midian seven years. The people of Israel lived in dens and caves in the mountains to hide from the Midianites. One day, the angel of the Lord appeared unto Gideon."

(Gideon is standing near several sheep, holding a staff.)

Angel: "The Lord is with you, mighty man of valour."

Gideon: "Who me? My family's poor, and I'm the youngest. I'm not a mighty man. But if the Lord is with us, why are we having so many problems?"

Angel: "You will save Israel from the Midianites. God has sent me to tell you this."

Gideon: "You're an angel from God, oh, no, *(Falls to his knees)* I'm going to die…!"

Angel: "Have peace, you will not die. God will be with you."

Gideon: "If I really am going to save Israel, and if you really are an angel, please let me see a sign from God. Then I will be brave, and I will believe."

Narrator: "And Gideon asked the Lord to give him a sign. He placed a fleece upon the ground. If the fleece was wet, and the ground was dry in the morning, then he promised to believe God's message."

(Servants come out and place the fleece on the ground. Another servant walks by with a sign for night, then a sign for morning.)

Gideon: "Servants, check the fleece. Is it wet?" *(Servants check the fleece, and nod their heads.)*

Servants: *(In unison)* "Yes, Master, the fleece is wet."

Gideon: "Servants, is the ground dry?" *(Servants feel of the ground and nod their heads.)*

Servants: *(In unison)* "Yes, Master, the ground is dry."

Narrator: "But Gideon was still afraid, and begged the Lord not to be angry with him. (*Gideon kneels as if in prayer.*) He asked for one more test. This time he asked for the ground to be wet, and the fleece to be dry." (*Gideon lies down on his mat or cot for the night.*)

(*Servant walks by with a sign for night, and then one for morning.*)

Gideon: "Servants, is the ground wet?" (*Servants feel of the ground and nod.*)

Servants: "Yes, Master the ground is wet."

Gideon: "Servants, is the fleece dry?" (*Servants feel the fleece and nod.*)

Servants: "Yes, Master, the fleece is dry."

Narrator: "So Gideon assembled his army for war. (*Soldiers gather around Gideon.*) But when they marched to the river, God spoke to him again." (*Children march around stage.*)

Angel: "Gideon, you have too many men in your army. I want you to send some of them home."

Gideon: "Too many men? This is a war, you know!"

Angel: "Send home those who are afraid."

Narrator: "So Gideon called his army together. He sent home those who were afraid. But still the Lord tested his faith." (*Gideon raises his hand while the narrator speaks. Some soldiers also raise their hands, and Gideon points to the door. They leave.*)

Angel: "Gideon, you have too many men in your army. I want you to send some more men home."

Gideon: "Too many men? Have you seen the size of that Midian army? I was scared before, but now I'm really terrified."

Angel: "Send home those who kneel down to drink. "

Narrator: "And when they reached the river, Gideon watched them drink. Those who bowed on their knees and drank directly from the stream were sent home. Those who scooped up water with their hands stayed to fight. Three hundred men were left. As the army approached the enemy camp, Gideon sneaked down to spy on the camp." (*As the narrator speaks, one by one the soldiers approach the edge of the stage. Some pretend to scoop up water in their hands. Gideon motions them to one side. Others kneel down to lap up water. Gideon motions them to leave.*)

Gideon: "Men, we are about to go to war with the Midianite army. But I think we need to find out more about our enemy before tomorrow. I will take some men with me, and we will sneak into the enemy camp. Then, when we get back, we will plan our attack."

(Gideon and the soldiers who were left sneak up on two soldiers sitting in front of their tent in the enemy camp. They look through binoculars at the camp.)

(Soldier One and Soldier Two are seated in front of their tent.)

Soldier One: "Man, I'm really scared."

Soldier Two: "Why would you be scared? We've got as many men as grains of sand by the sea. We're practically invincible."

Soldier One: "Just the same, I've got some weird feelings. I had the strangest dream last night, and it scared the pants right off me."

Soldier Two: "A dream? You're scared of a dream? What was it about?"

Soldier One: "There I was, minding my own business, getting my sword sharpened up for battle, and suddenly a cake of barley bread rolled into our camp."

Soldier Two: "You're scared of a loaf of bread?"

Soldier One: "Yep. When a loaf of bread rolls into camp, crushes a tent and kills everyone inside, you bet I'm afraid of it. I think we're in for some real trouble with those Israelites."

Soldier Two: "You might be right. That general Gideon has God on his side, and that's bad news for us. Even a huge army can't defeat God. Now you've done it, I'm getting the shakes just thinking about tomorrow." *(Gideon and his men shake hands and nod happily, giving each other "high fives" and then go offstage.)*

Narrator: "Then Gideon sneaked back to camp to get ready. He knew that God was going to help him. In the middle of the night, at midnight, he took his army on the attack. Each man carried only a trumpet and a lamp hidden inside a pitcher."

Gideon: "Men, here are your weapons." *(He hands each man a horn, a flashlight, and a plastic pitcher to hide the light in. The men stare at the items, then at each other, then at Gideon as if he was crazy.)*

Israelite Soldier: "Uh, Captain Gideon, sir?"

Gideon: "Yes, soldier. What is it?"

Israelite Soldier: "Are you sure you gave us the right weapons? They don't look very dangerous."

Gideon: "The Lord will fight for us. When I give the signal, blow your horns, break the pitchers, turn on the lights, and watch as God wins the battle! Let's go!"

(Gideon and soldiers sneak up on the tent. Gideon gives them a hand signal. They blow their horns and flash their lights. The enemy soldiers run away in terror.)

Gideon: "After them, men!" *(Gideon and the soldiers chase the enemy soldiers offstage.)*

(Steve and Dad come back onto stage)

Dad: "So, you see, God can help you just like he helped Gideon to be brave. I am reminded of a verse in the Bible, Isaiah 40:31. Say it with me: 'They they wait upon the Lord shall renew their strength. They shall mount up with wings as eagles, they shall run and not be weary, and they shall walk and not faint.'" *(Taken from the Holy Bible, King James Version.)*

(Children come out and sing "Teach Me, Lord to Wait")

SCENE IV: THE NIGHT OF THE PERFORMANCE

Narrator: "The night of the performance, everyone was on time. First, Brian came out to play his trumpet solo."

(Brian plays "Hark, the Herald Angels Sing"★)

Narrator: Next, a group of girls sang "The First Noel." *(A group of girls come out to sing the hymn.)*

Narrator: "Finally, it was Steve's turn to play his solo. He prayed, then approached the piano."

(Steve plays: "We Three Kings". Everyone applauds for him. He bows to the audience.)

Narrator: "And that was just the beginning. Steve learned to trust God more and more as the years went by."

★The hymns and songs suggested are found in most hymnals. Other Christmas songs may be substituted as desired. Also, students may play other instruments than those suggested, as well as adding more solos or performances as needed. The idea is that students are performing a Christmas program at their church. The number of performers can vary.

THE UNLIKELY HERO

• • • • • • • • • • • • • • • • •

THE UNLIKELY HERO

This is a play about mercy and forgiveness. At first, Jonah runs away from his responsibility, but he later repents and obeys God. Jonah learns that God's mercy is for everyone, even those who might seem unlovable.

Characters

Jonah
Ruth: A servant
Lord's Voice
Fisherman
Townsman 1
Townsman 2
Townswoman

Jonah's Wife
Benjamin: Jonah's friend
Sailor One
Sailor Two
Sailor Three
Several Townspeople

Props

- Fishing Pole
- Scrolls, and one piece of paper for a note
- Table with a few dishes on it
- Trunk or large chest
- Oversized hooded robe or coat
- Nets
- Money bag with coins
- Sideview of a boat (could be made from cardboard with small handles on the back)
- Sail (made from cloth attached to a tall lamp or flagpole with strings for rigging)
- Small bag with colored rocks in it (red, green, black, brown)
- Two oars
- Large fan to create wind during the storm
- Giant fish shape (made from painted cardboard or posterboard attached to a refrigerator box)
- Ribcage of a large fish (large enough for Jonah to sit behind as if in a jail cell)
- A tattered robe with seaweed or green strips attached
- White cream or face paint, white powder for Jonah's hair
- Several bundles
- Fishing line with several plastic fish on it
- Small fish head (taken from a toy fish)
- Large, leafy vine made from posterboard or painted cardboard
- Brown robes for sackcloth (a feedbag would work well with a string around the waist)
- Shower cap and slippers for Jonah's Wife
- Bundle of laundry for Ruth
- Sign with a decorated cake on it saying: "We miss you, Jonah."

THE UNLIKELY HERO

. . . .

SCENE I: THE COMMAND IS GIVEN

Benjamin: (*Enters carrying a fishing pole.*) "Hey, Jonah, I'm going fishin? You busy?"

Jonah: (*He is carrying several scrolls.*) "Yes, I'm preparing my sermon for the temple service next week."

Ben: "What's it about?"
Jonah: (*In a gruff voice*) "Repentin'."

Ben: "Oh, another tough one, eh? You always know how to hit 'em where it hurts." (*Makes a playful fist.*)

Jonah: "That's me, I like to tell it like it is. Repent, or get what's coming to you. That's my motto."

Ben: "Did you ever think of branching out, you know, trying something new? There are some verses in the Psalms about forgiveness, and love, and happy stuff like that."

Jonah: "I'll get around to those sometime, after I make sure everyone repents."

Ben: "Sure you don't want to go fishing instead?"

Jonah: "You know I don't like fish. See you at the service." (*Benjamin goes off.*)

Lord's Voice: "Jonah."

(*Jonah looks around, confused.*)

Lord's Voice: "Jonah."

(*Jonah looks up, then kneels down as if in prayer.*)

Jonah: "Yes, Lord."

Lord's Voice: "Jonah, you have been working hard on your sermon about repentance."

Jonah: "Oh, you like it? It's one of my better ones."

Lord's Voice: "Jonah, I want you to proclaim that sermon to a special group of people who really need to hear about repentance."

Jonah: (*excitedly*) "All right! (*He claps his hands together happily.*) Let me at 'em! Who are they?"

Lord's Voice: "I want you to go to Ninevah, that evil city, for I have seen their great wickedness, and you must warn them to change their ways."

Jonah: "Ninevah?...um..., yes..., well..., Ninevah....that's really far from here. I was just thinking of preaching around here. (*Points down to the ground in front of him.*) You see, I'm kind of a 'stay-at-home' prophet."

Lord's Voice: "I have told you what to do. Now go."

Jonah: "Are you sure? They're not my kind of people. They probably won't even listen to me anyway. Actually, I don't even like them. Nobody else likes them either."

(*Silence. Jonah looks up, then tries again.*)

Jonah: "Lord, are you listening? I don't want to go. Can't we talk about this? I think I feel sick. (*Touches his forehead as if feverish.*) "Look, a bump! It's probably chicken pox." (*Sighs*) "I guess He's gone. What am I going to do now?" (*He sighs, muttering under his breath "Ninevah...Of all the places...Ninevah" Jonah walks off, shaking his head.*)

SCENE II: SUSPICIOUS EVENTS

(*Scene opens with Jonah's wife and a servant girl, Ruth, clearing away the dinner dishes.*)

Wife: "Ruth, did you notice that Jonah seemed upset tonight? He hardly touched his food at dinner. He just sat there, mumbling, with a big frown on his face."

Ruth: "Yes, I thought that was strange. He usually loves roast lamb. And that pudding was delicious. You did a wonderful job preparing it."

Wife: "What do you think is wrong? Is he sick?"

Ruth: "I don't think so. He was humming a tune this morning."

Wife: "Huh... Well, something changed. "

Ruth: "Oh, I forgot to mention something. He was stuffing some things in a bag after dinner."

Wife: "Really? What kind of things?"

Ruth: "I couldn't see. He kept on turning around and hiding it from me while I was putting away the laundry. Very suspicious if you ask me."

Wife: (*Nodding.*) "Yes, suspicious indeed. I'll try to find out what's going on. Keep me posted if you see anything else unusual tonight."

Ruth: "You can count on me. (*salutes*) I love a good mystery."

(*Lights Dim. When lights come on, Wife rushes into the room, wearing a robe, shower cap and slippers.*)

Wife: "Ruth! Ruth! Where are you! Ruth! Emergency!" (*She bumps into Ruth, who is rushing toward her with an armful of laundry. They fall down, the laundry flies everywhere. Jonah's wife ends up with some of it on her head, but she doesn't seem to notice.*)

Ruth: (*Sitting in a pile of laundry.*) "What is it? Are you hurt?"

Wife: "It's Jonah! He's gone! Call the police. Call 9-1-1. Call somebody!"

Benjamin: (*Comes rushing in*) "Did someone call for help? I was just passing by. I heard someone yelling....Hey, what happened to you two?"

Wife: "He must have left in the night. When I woke up, he was gone!"

Benjamin: "Who?"

Ruth: "Jonah's gone. Have you seen him?"

Benjamin: "No, but why is that trunk open? It's usually locked." (*Points to a large chest.*)

Wife: (*Looks in the trunk and gasps.*) "That ugly robe is gone! It's way too big and has a giant hood that covers his whole face. No one will even recognize him with that on."

Ruth: "Maybe he doesn't want anyone to recognize him. Maybe he's running away from home.... to... join the circus!"

Wife: "The circus! And he didn't even take a sandwich with him. Oh, my, this is very strange."

Benjamin: "Wait! What's that? (*Pointing down inside the trunk.*) It's a note! (*He picks up a small sheet of parchment and hands it to Jonah's wife.*)

Wife: (*Reading from the page.*) "Dear Wife: Gone on vacation. Don't call me, and don't look for me at Ninevah, 'cause I won't be there. Don't worry about me. Love, Jonah."

Ruth: (*Looking puzzled.*). "Vacation! Ninevah? It doesn't make sense."

Benjamin: "C'mon, let's check around town. Maybe someone saw him leave." (*They leave.*)

SCENE III: THE RUNAWAY PROPHET

(*Scene opens with three sailors putting some nets into a boat. Jonah approaches, whispers to Sailor One. He walks over to consult with his fellow sailors.*)

Sailor One: "This guy wants to book passage with us." (*Points to Jonah, whose face is hidden under a large hood.*)

Sailor Two: "Who is he?"

Sailor One: "I couldn't understand what he said. He mumbled something that sounded like …uh… Fred."

Sailor Two: "Fred? I've never heard of a name like that. Should we let him go with us? He looks dangerous to me. He'll probably rob us in our sleep."

Sailor One: "Rob us? Look at that money bag he's carrying. He doesn't need to rob anybody."

Sailor Three: "Yeah, and my wife said I'd better bring her back something good this trip. She's getting tired of eating dried up figs. I need some money. After all, how much trouble can one man be anyway?"

Sailor Two: "All right, but I'm going to be watching him all the way to Tarshish. There's something strange about that fellow."

34

Sailor One: (*Motions to Jonah*) "Come aboard. You'll have to pay double because we don't usually take passengers on such short notice." (*Jonah hands him a money purse that jingles. The sailor shakes it a bit, then smiles at the others and Jonah steps into the ship.*)

(*Jonah goes to the back of the boat and lies down. Sailors create a rocking effect by pulling on handles attached to the back of the cardboard boat shape. The boat begins rocking, and a large fan blows hard against the sail.*)

Sailor One: (*Pulling on the rigging of a sail*). "It's gettin' pretty bad. I can hardly hold this line."

Sailor Two: (*Yelling over the wind.*) "I've never seen a storm this bad."

Sailor Three: "I think we'd better pray for help. We'll never keep the ship afloat in this storm."

(*The three sailors bow their heads and begin to pray loudly, "Help us, great gods of wind and sea...don't let us die!" Nothing changes. The wind continues to blow even harder.*)

Sailor Two: "It didn't work. We'd better throw some stuff out! We're going to sink!"

(*The sailors begin tossing bundles over the side as the boat continues to rock. As they lift bundles from the back of the boat, they notice Jonah, still sleeping.*)

Sailor Three: "Look at him! Still sleeping! Is he deaf?"

Sailor One: "You there! (*Kicks at Jonah.*) "Sleeper….Fred….whatever your name is…..Wake up!"

Jonah: (Sits up, yawning, then looks around angrily.) "What do you want?"

Sailor Two: "Pray…Pray to your God….If He doesn't help us, we're all going to die!"

(*Jonah waves them off and lays back down as if he doesn't care. The sailors leave him and decide to cast lots.*)

Sailor One: "This is not just any storm. Somebody's god is angry. Let's figure out who it is. I've got some stones right here! We'll use them to find out whose fault this is."

(*He takes out four stones from a pouch on his belt. The sailors discuss which stone is theirs.*)

Sailor One: "I'll take the green one. You all pick one."

Sailor Two: "There's a black one in there. I don't want that one. Give me the red one."

Sailor Three: "Well, I'm not taking the black one either. Give that to the Sleeper. If anyone's in trouble, it's probably him. Give me the brown one."

Sailor One: "I'll throw the stones down. The one that lands farthest away from the center is the one chosen."

(He shakes up his bag of stones, then dumps then on the boat floor. They all bend over to look and say together, "The black one!" Then they all turn to look at Jonah, who is sitting up, watching from his seat in the back of the boat.)

Jonah: *(Rolling his eyes.)* "I know, I know. It's me."

Sailor Two: "Your name isn't Fred, is it? Who are you? Where are you from? What have you done to us?"

Jonah: *(He stands)* "I am Jonah, the Hebrew prophet. *(Points upward, then sweeps his arm toward the sea.)* My God is the True God, the One who made land and sea, the Ruler of everything. I disobeyed Him and He's angry with me." *(Points to himself.)*

Sailor One: "What are we going to do with you? We have to do something, or we'll all die. Tell us, what will satisfy your God?"

Jonah: "Throw me into the sea. There's nothing else to do. I must put my life into His hands, and pray for mercy."

Sailor Three: "I don't want to throw anyone over. Let's try and row for it."

(The sailors take up oars and try to row, but the wind still rages. Jonah stands with arms folded in the back of the boat, unmoving. One drops his oar, then the others do the same.)

Sailor Two: "It's hopeless. We can't even move at all! We're all dead men!"

Jonah: *(Standing with arms folded.)* "I told you so. You have to throw me in if you want to live. I'm not jumpin' in by myself."

Sailor Two: "It looks like he's going to have to walk the plank after all."

Sailor One: *(Looks upward and prays.)* "O, God of the Hebrews, forgive us. We don't want to kill anyone. Please don't blame us for this man's troubles. *(He turns, points to Jonah.)* Throw him overboard, men!"

(*From behind the ship, a giant fish appears. After they throw Jonah off the back of the boat, the sailors kneel down as if they are looking down into the water. Jonah runs across the stage, moving his arms as if he is swimming, with the fish following him. As it gets near to him the sailors call out* "Look out behind you!" *Jonah looks back and says,* "Uh-Oh!" *The fish catches up to him and they both disappear offstage. Sailor Two calls out in a sing-song voice* "Sor-ry." *The lights dim.*)

SCENE IV: INSIDE THE BELLY OF THE FISH

(*Scene opens with Jonah looking out from between the giant ribs of the fish, as if looking out through the bars of a jail cell. His clothing is mere rags, his hair has turned white as well as his skin. He looks like a ghost.*)

Jonah: "Well, here I am in a fish's belly. He gulped me down like I was a goldfish cracker! I hope I tasted good! I wonder if they're missing me at home. Right now, Benjamin is probably fishin' on the lake. Too bad he can't reel me in right now." (*Benjamin appears at the side of the stage, casting his fishing line out and reeling it in.*)

Jonah: "And my wife is probably baking a cake for me that says, "We miss you, Jonah." (*Wife appears on other side of stage, holding up a picture of a cake with those words on it.*)

Jonah: "It's been three long days since the 'All You Can Eat: Jonah Buffet' happened. I don't smell so good either. Ruth is going be mad when she sees this robe. ((*Holds up his arm to show his tattered clothing. Ruth appears, carrying a robe which she lays out and smooths with her hands.*) "Look at me now. Swimmin' with stinky fish heads. There goes another one." (*He holds up a fish head, makes a face and throws it.*)

Jonah: "The Lord saved me, I have to admit it. I was going down forever when this fish swallowed me. I disobeyed God, but He didn't kill me. God…God…You are great and I am small. I should have obeyed You, but I ran. Lord, if you will just let me out of here, and let me live, I promise I will obey You. I will go to those evil Ninevites and I'll tell them to repent. If only I could get out of here …Lord?....Lord? …Can you hear me?...I'm sorry…Hey, what's happening?"

(*The fish begins to shake. Jonah crouches, swaying back and forth. Suddenly he rolls out from behind the ribs of the fish onto the ground.*)'

Lord's Voice: "Now, Jonah, GO, and preach what I have told you to say."

Jonah: "Yes, Lord, I will go."

(*He stands up, brushing the bits of seaweed from his tattered, filthy robe. A fisherman walks over to him, holding several fish on a line.*)

Fisherman: "What happened to you! Why are you so white? And where's all your hair?" (*He plugs his nose.*)

Jonah: (*He walks steadily toward the man, pointing his finger into the man's face as he shouts the words*). "REPENT! REPENT OF YOUR SIN, OR ELSE YOU WILL DIE!"

(*The fisherman backs away, trips and falls. As he crawls backward from the white-faced prophet, Jonah asks him a question.*)

Jonah: (*Speaking fiercely.*) "Which way to Ninevah?" (*The frightened man points. Jonah stalks away, saying,* "REMEMBER, REPENT OR ELSE YOU WILL DIE! He disappears offstage. The fisherman runs off in the opposite direction.*)

SCENE V: THE TOWN OF NINEVAH

(*Scene opens with several townspeople standing around a table. Two townsmen are seated at the table. A servant is attempting to serve their food.*)

Townsman 1: "Hey, watch it! You spilled some of that juice on my new tunic. What's the matter, can't you pour straight?" (*He pushes the servant, spilling some liquid onto the floor.*)

Townsman 2: "Pay attention, would you? I didn't order lentils, he did." (*He pushes his plate off onto the floor. The townspeople laugh. The servant bends down to clean up the mess.*)

Townswoman: "Look! Over there! Someone's coming! He looks angry." (*Jonah approaches the crowd.*)

Townsman 1: "So what? We'll give him something to think about if he tries to……hey, who *is that?* What's wrong with his face?" (*The townspeople murmur and back away from Jonah as he approaches. He looks angry, and is still wearing his rags covered with slime and seaweed.*)

Jonah: (*Walks right up to the man and puts his face close to him.*) "REPENT! REPENT OR ELSE YOU WILL DIE! (*He sweeps his arm around to include all in the crowd.*) "All of you! God has seen your wickedness, and He has sent ME to tell you that He is going to destroy you. You will all die, and your city will crumble into dust. You've only got forty days to live. FORTY DAYS! REPENT!"

(*Jonah walks away, repeating his message,* "Forty days. Forty days left to live. Repent, or die in forty days. Only forty days to live…Forty days…" *The people fall to their knees, frightened.*")

Townswoman: "Forty days? Oh no…"

Townspeople: "God, help us. Forgive us. We are sorry for our sins. Please don't destroy us."

(Lights dim. When lights go up again, Jonah is seated on one side of the platform under a large leafy vine. The townspeople are kneeling on the stage, wearing brown sackcloth, praying quietly. A couple of them begin to sing, Amazing Grace, How Sweet the Sound… As the verse ends, they quiet down to a whisper of voices praying.)

Jonah: *(Speaking from his seat under the vine.)* "Look at them down there… Repenting! I don't believe it! I've been waiting here for God to destroy them, but He didn't. I knew it! That's why I didn't want to come here in the first place. Good thing this vine grew up here to give me shade while I wait for the hammer to fall on them."

(As Jonah sits there, the plant begins to shrink. It continues to shrink down until it disappears.)

Jonah: "Oh, man, now my vine is gone. The sun's gettin' hot. I think I feel a blister on my head. *(He feels the top of his head.)* Somebody turn on the air conditioning!"

Lord's Voice: "Jonah, are you really right to be angry about the vine?"

Jonah: "Well…maybe…"

Lord's Voice: "That vine grew up in only one day. You didn't plant it or tend it. You've never even seen it before. There are twenty-six thousand people in that town who don't even understand the difference between right and wrong. I have loved them, and cared for them all these years. Should I have saved the vine, and killed the people instead?"

Jonah: *(Bows his head)* "Oh, Lord, I am ashamed of myself. You forgave me when I ran away, and I must learn to forgive others."

Lord's Voice: "Now, go down there and teach them about My love. Show them how to live in righteous ways."

DANGER IN THE DEN

DANGER IN THE DEN: A PUPPET SHOW

"Danger in the Den" is a puppet show about the story of Daniel in the Lions' Den. The lions are hungry, and the evil advisors are devising a plan to have Daniel thrown to the lions.

Characters:

Narrator	King Darius
Lion 1	Guard 1
Lion 2	Guard 2
Lion 3	Daniel
Advisor 1	Angel
Advisor 2	
Advisor 3	

(One or two people needed for props and changing of scenes)

Props:

- Puppets needed:
- Three Lions
- King Darius
- Two Guards
- Daniel
- Three advisors
- Two Guards
- Angel
- Narrator
- Light bulb poster (One side has a lighted bulb, the other side a burned-out bulb)
- Notepad or clipboard and pencil
- Toy mouse mounted on a stick
- Mirror
- Sign that says "Kill Daniel, Sign Here"
- Giant question mark
- Scroll for the law
- Tissues
- One slipper with a hole in the sole
- Background scenery for a lions' den, a throne room, and Daniel's home.
- Balloon

DANGER IN THE DEN: A PUPPET SHOW

SCENE I: THE LIONS ARE HUNGRY

(Narrator enters and waves to the audience.)

Narrator: "Hello! I'm so glad you're here. I just have to tell someone…There's an evil plan afoot in Babylon. Would you like to hear about it? Ok, but…Beware! There will be danger…(*Puppet looks from side to side as if ready to share a secret*) Hold on to your seats, we're about to enter…the lions' den!"

(Lion 1 enters)

LION 1: *(big yawn)* "I'm tired of eating scrawny, stinky mice. The king hasn't thrown anyone in here for days."

(Lions 2 and 3 enter. Lion 2 is chewing on a rubber mouse.)

LION 2: *(Gulps loudly. The mouse disappears.)* "I'm so hungry I could eat two elephant burgers and a side order of zebra fries."

LION 3: *(Puts his face close to Lion 2)* "Well, would you settle for one…big…juicy…and very unlucky…person? Mmmmmm?"

LION 2: "What makes you think we're finally going to eat a person?"

LION 3: "Oh, I have my ways…Ha ha ha ha ha!"

LION 1: "Well, tell us…Who? (tips his head from side to side like a clock ticking as he says each word) When? Where? How?"

LION 3: "That's a lot of questions. I only have one answer…it's Daniel!"

LION 2: *(nodding)* "Oh, Daniel. I heard that no one likes him, except the king." *(growl)*

LION 1: *(shakes his head)* "Don't interrupt his story. After all, he's got his ways."
(Lions 1 and 2 laugh loudly and roar)

LION 3: *(puckers up his face angrily)* "Ahem" (*He waits for them to stop laughing.*)
"As I was saying…Daniel is in big trouble."

LION 1: "Oh, yeah. He thinks he's the cat's meow."

LION 3: "Yeah, but really soon, he's going to be Meow Mix for lions! Here kitty, kitty, kitty….it's Dinnertime." (*Lion 1 bites Lion 3 on the mane and shakes him up. All lions roar and laugh loudly.*)

LION 2: "Shhhhhhhhhh. I hear someone coming."

LION 1: "Let's listen. Maybe we can find out about tomorrow's menu."

(*All lions duck out of sight.*)

SCENE II: SECRET PLANS

NARRATOR: "Are they gone?" (*Looks around nervously*) "Ooooooooo…those lions sound hungry. Did you hear them roaring? It gives me the willies when they do that. (*shivers and trembles*) Uh-oh, here come the advisors. I hear they're really sneaky. Don't believe a word they say." (*hurries offstage*)

(*In the palace. Advisors enter.*)

ADVISOR 1: "That Daniel…he's reaaaaaaaaaally bugging me."

ADVISOR 2: "Yeah, he's annoying all right. The king even invited him over for Camel Pot Pie, my favorite."

ADVISOR 3: "*I* should be the favorite because of my super good looks." (*holds up a mirror and admires himself*)

ADVISOR 1: (*spoken in an evil voice*) "I've got a plan to get rid of Daniel forever."

ADVISOR 3: (*sighing*) "Well, it better be a good one."

ADVISOR 2: "I've got a plan, too."

ADVISOR 1: "Let me say my plan first." (*He whacks the other puppet*)

ADVISOR 2: (*whacks him back*) "Mine's better."

ADVISOR 3: (*pushing them apart*) "How do you know? He hasn't even said the plan yet."

ADVISOR 1: "As I was saying, I have a plan."

ADVISOR 2: "Ooooooooooo…He has a plan."

ADVISOR 3: "Shhhhhhhhhhhhhhh. Now you behave!"

ADVISOR 1: "I'm going to ask the king to sign this paper." (*He holds up a sign that reads "Kill Daniel. Sign Here." An arrow points to the line.*)

ADVISOR 2: (*Laughs so hard he falls down.*)

ADVISOR 1: (*after the laughing stops*) "What's so funny?"

ADVISOR 3: "You can't *tell* the king we want to kill Daniel."

ADVISOR 1: "Well, we do, don't we?"

ADVISOR 2: "Listen, We have to be sneaky, sly, crafty...like a fox...sort of like...me!"

ADVISOR 3: (*makes a face at Advisor 2*) "Yes, well...We have to get rid of him without looking like we want to get rid of him. Get it?"

ADVISOR 1: (*A large question mark appears over his head*) "Nope."

ADVISOR 3: "I'll tell the king he's sooooooo handsome and soooooooooo smart that everyone should pray to the king and no one else."

ADVISOR 1: (*Question mark appears again*) "That's nice, but what does that have to do with Daniel?"

ADVISOR 2: (*hopping up and down*) "I know! I know!" (*A giant light bulb appears over his head.*) "We'll make a special paper about it."

ADVISOR 1: "Way cool. What kind of paper? I know how to make paper airplanes, with the wings...and..."

ADVISOR 2: "No, no, no...A paper about a new law, of course! Anyone who disobeys the law will be thrown to the lions."

ADVISOR 1: "Daniel won't break the law. All he ever does is pray by his window. Hey... wait a minute...(*The giant light bulb moves over behind him*)....If Daniel prays to God instead of the king, we'll charge over and kill him!" (*The light bulb sign flips around to the back and shows a burned-out bulb.*)

ADVISOR 3: "No, No! *We* aren't going to kill *anybody*. We're the good guys, remember? We'll make the king do it. I'll write up a law and we'll get the king to sign it."

ADVISOR 2: "And just how will you get the king to sign that?"

ADVISOR 3: "Just leave that to me."

ADVISOR 1: "And when Daniel starts to pray again….."

Everyone together shouts: "LION MEAT!"

(All laugh loudly, then exit)

SCENE III: IN THE THRONE ROOM

NARRATOR: "Oh, no! It looks like curtains for Daniel! *(Paces around)* "Oh, my, this is terrible news. What do you think Daniel will do? Oh my, oh my, oh my…" *(He rushes off.)*

(Scene opens in the king's throne room.)

KING DARIUS: "Guards!"

(2 guards appear. Guard 2 has a list and a pen.)

GUARD 1: "Yes, your Majesty."

KING: "Who's waiting to see me today?"

GUARD 2: *(Holding up a list)* "Let's see…there are some shepherds who were caught stealing sheep…"

KING: "Stealing is bad. Throw them to the lions." *(Guard 2 scribbles on the list.)*

GUARD 1: "Then there's this guy who won't pay his taxes."

KING: "That's even worse. Lions again." *(Guard 2 scribbles on the list again.)*

GUARD 1: "After that, there's a minister from Egypt to argue about land…"

KING: "EEEEEW! Definitely lions!" *(Guard 2 scribbles on the list again.)*

GUARD 1: "Then Daniel, your advisor, will be coming in after lunch."

GUARD 2: *(Holding his pen ready to write)* "Lions for him?"

KING: "Of course not! Are you crazy? He's the best advisor I've ever had. If anyone dares to lay a finger on Daniel, I'll…I'll…well…I'll turn them into Lion MacNuggets!"

GUARD 1: "Is that all for today, sire?"

KING: "Is there anyone else on the list?"

GUARD 2: "Let me see…(*looking over the list*) Yes, there are three advisors begging to see you."

KING: (*shaking his head in despair*) "Oh, no, they're always whining, and I can't throw them to the lions because they're my relatives. Can't you chase after them…or something?"

GUARD 1: "We did that yesterday, sire. And now they're back again."

KING: (*sighing loudly*) "Oh well, show them in."

(*Guards leave. Advisors enter. They bow and wait to be called.*)

KING: "Yes, yes, approach the throne…if you must." (*Mumbles under his breath,* "Whiners")

ADVISOR 2: "You're looking fantastic today, King Darius!"

(*King makes a confused face.*)

ADVISOR 3: "I agree. And I should know. I'm an excellent judge of how people look." (*Holds up the mirror briefly, admiring himself*)

ADVISOR 1: "Yes, you must be eating all your vegetables, like onions… brussel sprouts… cabbage…broccoli…turnips…parsnips…." (*Advisor 1 bumps him and says* "Shhhhhhhh!")

(*King makes another confused face. Turning toward the audience, he speaks*)

King: "Something fishy's going on here."

ADVISOR 2: "Perhaps in the past we may have caused a teensy-weensy bit of trouble, but please let us make it up to you."

ADVISOR 3: "We want to give you a party, O Magnificent King!" (*Holds up a balloon*)

KING: (*in a suspicious voice*) "Really? What kind of a party?"

ADVISOR 3: "A really big one. After all, you are the greatest king of all time."

KING: *(nodding)* "That's true."

(Advisors repeat after him like an echo) "Too true. Too true."

ADVISOR 3: "People need to know how great you really are. We'll write up a law so that everyone will pray to you, great king."

(Advisor 3 holds up the mirror so the king can admire himself.)

KING: "Radical idea."

ADVISORS: *(in unison)* "Radical."

ADVISOR 2: "And if someone disobeys your new law, O King…"

KING: "Who would?"

ADVISOR 1: "I know someone who…." *(Advisor 2 grabs him and covers him mouth before he can say anything else)*

ADVISOR 3: "I have the paper right here."

KING: "Yes, it sounds great. Let me sign it."

ADVISOR 2: "Never mind the fine print at the bottom."

KING: "No, no, I haven't got time to read that. Give me the paper."

(ADVISOR 3 hands him the paper. King signs.)

KING: "I may change my mind about you three after all. Now run along and get my party ready."

(Advisors leave, giggling to themselves.)

SCENE IV: DANIEL'S ARREST

NARRATOR: "The King has been tricked! I never would have believed it. I hope Daniel is watching out for spies. If they catch him…*(He shudders)*…it's too scary for words. It doesn't look like there's much hope for Daniel. Boo-Hoo." (*He grabs a tissue and blows his nose loudly*). "I can't bear to watch. Oh, no, there go the guards."

(*Narrator exits, sobbing and wailing.*)

DANIEL: "Dear God, I thank You for this day. I thank You for my food, and for all You have done for me. I pray that You will help me to show these people how to worship You as the One True God."

(*There is a knock at the door. Two guards enter.*)

GUARD 1: "Daniel of the Israelites, you're under arrest, by royal decree."

DANIEL: "What have I done?"

GUARD 2: "No one is allowed to pray to anyone except the king."

DANIEL: "But I always pray to God right here, right in this very window. The King knows that."

GUARD 1: "Not anymore. Anyone caught praying is under arrest."

GUARD 2: "Now come quietly."

DANIEL: "I'm sure the King will understand."

(*The Guards escort Daniel offstage.*)

(*Guards enter the throne room with Daniel.*)

KING: "Guards, why have you arrested Daniel? Release him at once."

GUARD 1: "But, your Majesty….we are only obeying orders."

KING: "Whose orders?"

GUARD 2: "Your orders, Sire."

GUARD 1: "Your new law states that no one can worship anyone but you."

KING: "I've been tricked by those whiners! Give me the law. Let me read it again."

(*Guard 1 hands him the paper*)

KING: (*mumbling to himself*) "There must be a way…."

KING: (*throwing down the paper*) "I won't do it. I won't throw him to the lions. I don't care about the law!"

GUARD 1: "But then, O King, everyone will call you a liar. You'll be the laughingstock of the whole kingdom."

GUARD 2: "You know you have to do it. It's a law now."

KING: "O, Daniel, I'm so sorry. I never wanted to get you in trouble. I have to throw you to the lions. Why did you have to pray?"

DANIEL: "Do not fear, Great King. God will take care of me."

KING: "I hope so." (*Sighs*) "Take him away. May your God watch over you, Daniel."

(*The Guards lead Daniel away.*)

SCENE V: DANIEL IN THE LION'S DEN

NARRATOR: "Daniel's been captured. He's a lion lunchable for sure. Ohhhhhhhhh." (*sobs, then blows nose with a tissue*) "I can't believe the evil advisors are going to get their way. Daniel prayed a lot. I don't know why God didn't save him. But there's still time. Maybe He will. I sure hope so. I'm running out of tissues." (*blows nose loudly again and goes offstage.*)

(*In the Den*)

LION 3: "Well, well, have you heard the news?"

LION 2: "Who gets news around here? My cable TV has been shut off for months."

LION 1: "Is this a game? Can we guess? Does it start with "A" for appetizers?"

LION 3: "No, it's not a game. We're going to eat somebody famous."

LION 2: "It's probably somebody who lost his head and disobeyed the king."

LION 1: "I don't care if he has a head. I never eat that part anyway."

(*Lions laugh*)

LION 3: "Actually, the unlucky person is named Daniel."

LION 2: "I knew it all along."

LION 1: "I'm getting some salt ready."

LION 2: "I smell something. I think it's Dinner Time."

(Lions growl and crouch down. Daniel appears in the midst of the lions.)

(Lions growl and creep toward Daniel. He looks up to heaven and prays.)

DANIEL: "O God, You are a great God. I know that You will protect me."

(Angel appears and touches each lion's mouth.)

DANIEL: "Thank you, God, for watching over me."

SCENE VI: THE KING'S REVENGE

NARRATOR: "Did you see that angel appear out of nowhere? Weren't you surprised? I guess I should have had more faith. I was so worried last night that I got a hole in my slippers from pacing the floor." *(Holds up a slipper with a hole.)* "I wonder how the king slept last night."

(King comes on stage alone. He paces back and forth.)

KING: "What a terrible night. I didn't sleep a wink. Look at this hole in my slippers! *(Holds up a slipper with a hole)* "I'm so worried about Daniel. I must hurry to the den and see if he's all right."

(King hurries off. Lions enter, with Daniel in the middle of them. King calls from offstage)

KING: "Daniel, Daniel, did you survive? Are you all right? Did your God save you?"

DANIEL: "Yes, King Darius, I'm fine. My God is very powerful."

KING: "Guards, get him out of there."

(Lions disappear. King comes on stage and hugs Daniel.)

KING: "Never again will I be tricked by those whiners. Your God is the real God. I will make a new law, and everyone will bow to Daniel's God."

DANIEL: "Thank you, King."

(*Daniel leaves.*)

KING: "Guards, get me those tricksters."

(*King goes offstage.*)

KING: (*from offstage*) "You've tricked me for the last time. Throw them in!"

(*Three lions pop up, holding the wiggling advisors in their mouths.*)

ADVISOR 3: "Oh, my hair is getting messed up!"

ADVISOR 2: "Can't we talk this over?"

ADVISOR 1: "Ouch! That's my leg you're chewing on. I need that!"

(*Lions take the advisors with them offstage.*)

NARRATOR: "Wow! What an adventure! I was on the edge of my seat the whole time. I should have known God wouldn't let Daniel down. Isn't God wonderful? Well, I hope you liked our story. Good-bye."